LIVING THINGS
and
A Compare and Contrast Book
NONLIVING THINGS

by Kevin Kurtz

Everywhere you go,
you will see
living things.

Everywhere you go,
you will see
nonliving things.

Living things

How are they different from each other?

Are living things
the only things
that move?

Not necessarily.
Some nonliving things move . . .

. . . while some living things cannot.

Are living things the only things that grow and change?

All living things do
grow and change.

But some nonliving things
grow and change too.

Are living things the only things that reproduce?

Do only living
things make
babies?

Or seeds?

Or copies of
themselves?

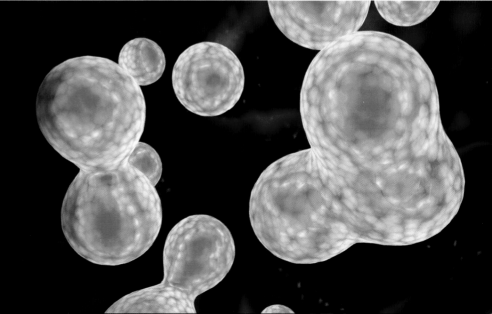

Some nonliving things can
also make copies of themselves.

And though almost all living things can reproduce . . .

. . . some living things, like mules and male ligers, cannot.

Are living things the only things that need food?

That need water and breathe oxygen?

All living things do need energy, nutrients, and water to exist. Many of them also need to breathe oxygen to exist.

But, this nonliving thing also needs "food" and oxygen to exist.

This nonliving thing cannot exist without always getting water from its environment.

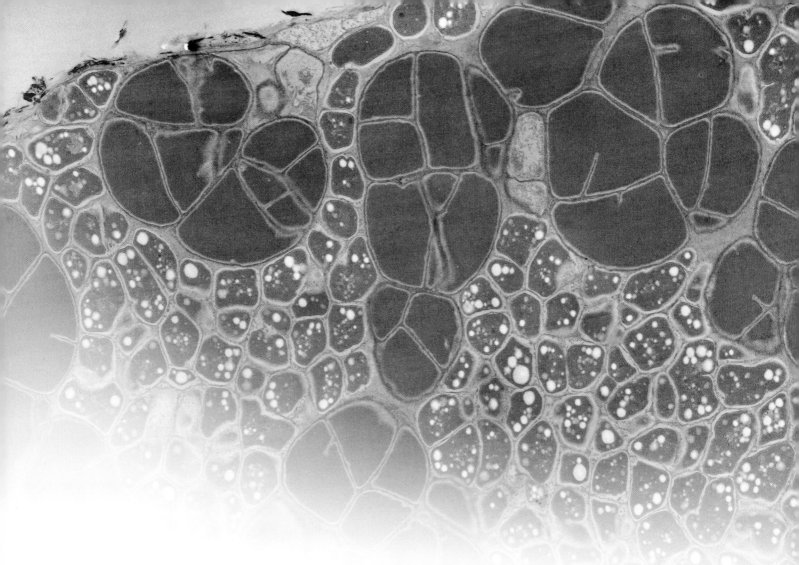

And some living things, like these microbes, are poisoned by oxygen. They breathe other things, like sulphur and even iron.

So how are living things
different from nonliving things?

Not even scientists have a
perfect answer.

But if something does ALL these things, then it is probably a living thing.

Breathe.

Drink Water.

Take energy and nutrients from its environment.

Reproduce.

Grow and change.

For Creative Minds

Glossary

Breathe: to take in and push out a gas

Energy: the ability to do work. Work can be anything something does, like move, think, grow, or reproduce.

Environment: a system made of living and nonliving things

Grow: to change, develop, or get bigger

Reproduce: to make a copy or a new thing like itself

What are some living things in your environment? Nonliving things?

People take in gas from their environment. They take in oxygen and push out carbon dioxide.

Plants take in gas from their environment. They take in carbon dioxide and push out oxygen.

What do you do that takes energy? How do you get energy from things in your environment?

Some nonliving things are not yet living things, or used to be living things but aren't any more. Which of the following was or will be a living thing?

- a mummy
- a marble statue
- frog eggs
- a painting of a person
- dinosaur bones
- a video of a cat
- petrified wood

If you make a drawing of a person, is that reproduction?

Answers: Was or will be a living thing: a mummy, frog eggs, dinosaur bones, petrified wood. Never a living thing: a marble statue, a painting of a person, a video of a cat

Living or Nonliving Checklist

Do you think this thing is living or nonliving? A living thing will meet most or all of the criteria on this checklist. For a printable version of this checklist, see the Teaching Activities at www.ArbordalePublishing.com.

bear

- ✓ Breathes
- ✓ Takes in water
- ✓ Gets nutrients and energy from its environment
- ✓ Reproduces
- ✓ Grows and changes

giraffe

- ? Breathes
- ? Takes in water
- ? Gets nutrients and energy from its environment
- ? Reproduces
- ? Grows and changes

penguin

- ? Breathes
- ? Takes in water
- ? Gets nutrients and energy from its environment
- ? Reproduces
- ? Grows and changes

Living: bear, penguin, giraffe. Nonliving: none

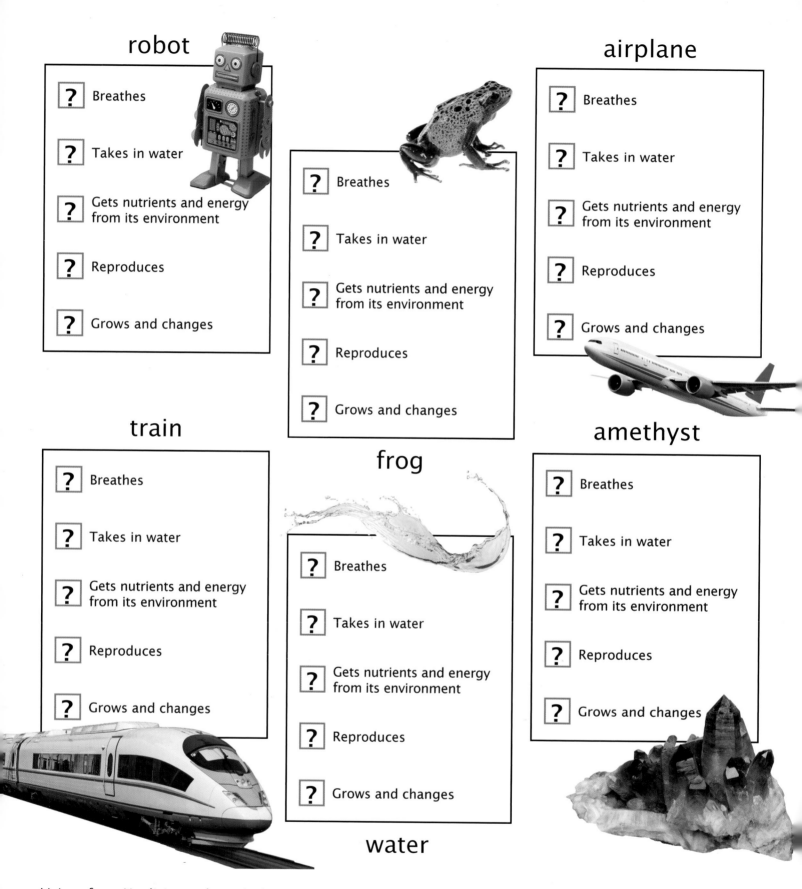

robot

? Breathes

? Takes in water

? Gets nutrients and energy from its environment

? Reproduces

? Grows and changes

airplane

? Breathes

? Takes in water

? Gets nutrients and energy from its environment

? Reproduces

? Grows and changes

? Breathes

? Takes in water

? Gets nutrients and energy from its environment

? Reproduces

? Grows and changes

train

? Breathes

? Takes in water

? Gets nutrients and energy from its environment

? Reproduces

? Grows and changes

frog

amethyst

? Breathes

? Takes in water

? Gets nutrients and energy from its environment

? Reproduces

? Grows and changes

? Breathes

? Takes in water

? Gets nutrients and energy from its environment

? Reproduces

? Grows and changes

water

Living: frog. Nonliving: robot, airplane, train, water, amethyst